Life's Challenges

SAYING GOOD-BYE TO UNCLE JOE

What to Expect When Someone You Love Dies

by Nancy Loewen

illustrated by Christopher Lyles

PICTURE WINDOW BOOKS

a capstone imprint

Today would have been Uncle Joe's birthday.

Last year, Aunt Kay threw Uncle Joe a surprise party. We had *so* much fun! We ate cake and batted around balloons. All the cousins got a piggyback ride—even Charlie, the biggest.

"See, I've still got it," Uncle Joe said. "Over the hill, my foot!"

That was in February.

In April, we got the phone call.

I heard Mom say hello. Then she said, **"Oh, no!"** Her voice didn't sound like her at all. Mom and Dad talked in their bedroom. I could hear Mom crying. My skin started feeling all prickly.

5

After a few minutes, Mom and Dad sat us down in the living room. **"We have some sad news for you,"** Dad said. **"This afternoon, Uncle Joe had a stroke. I'm afraid he ... he died."**

Learning of a loved one's death can be very startling. Even if the death was expected, the news can still come as a shock.

"But we just saw him a couple of days ago," I said. Every Sunday night, Uncle Joe and Aunt Kay came to our house for ice cream and card games. I looked forward to our Sunday sundaes all week. "He can't be dead!"

Mom started to cry again. So did my brothers. Dad cleared his throat. I just lay there. I didn't know what to do.

A lot happened in the next few days. Mom and Dad were busy. Grandma and Grandpa stayed at our house. People came to visit. The phone rang so much I just stopped hearing it.

Aunt Kay stayed with us too. I gave her my bed and my big pillow that looks like a heart with arms. She hugged me tight. **"You are such a comfort,"** she told me.

The days following a death are busy ones. Families need to plan a funeral or memorial service. They need to make arrangements for burial or cremation. Sometimes they need to travel. Connecting with others can make it all a little easier.

Mom asked if I wanted to go to the visitation.
At first I said no. I was scared. I'd never
seen a dead person before. But then
I changed my mind. Uncle Joe had
told me I was the bravest kid he
knew. If he said I was brave,
then I was.

JOE

Remember, you're brave, I told myself when I reached the casket. The body inside *looked* like Uncle Joe. He had Uncle Joe's glasses and that funny scar on his forehead.

But he didn't *seem* like Uncle Joe. Not really. Something was missing.

For many people, seeing a loved one's body is an important part of saying good-bye. It helps them accept that the person has died.

At the church the next morning, my whole family sat together up front. There were songs and readings. I didn't understand it all. But I liked hearing people say nice things about Uncle Joe.

The burial was the hardest part. Everyone cried. I cried too. When we left the cemetery, it felt like we were leaving Uncle Joe behind.

What happens to us after we die? Does a part of us live on in some way? Different religions answer these questions in different ways. Many people are comforted by their belief in heaven or another kind of afterlife.

After the funeral, we spent a lot of time with Aunt Kay. But we stopped having Sunday sundaes. Our Sunday nights didn't feel special anymore.

At different times after a death, you might feel scared, angry, lonely, or simply sad. You might feel perfectly fine one day and upset the next. Grief is different for everyone. There's no right way or wrong way to grieve.

At school, I had a hard time finishing my work. Once, I pinched my finger in my desk. Even though it didn't hurt much, I acted like it did. I think I just wanted to cry.

One day Dad was late picking me up from art class.

"Where were you?" I yelled. "You were supposed to be here 10 minutes ago! I was waiting for you, and you weren't here!"

Dad said he was sorry for being late. Then he asked if I was worried something was going to happen to him or Mom.

"It's true that everyone dies at some point," he said. "But it's not very likely that Mom or I will die while you're growing up."

He held his finger so it was almost touching his thumb. **"There's only *this* much of a chance. See? It's so tiny, it's not something you need to worry about."**

I felt better after that.

When someone you love dies, you might be afraid that other people in your life will die too. Or you might have questions that no one has answered. Talking about your fears with a parent, teacher, or other adult you trust can make them easier to deal with.

School let out for the summer.

Some things were the way they'd always been. I took swimming lessons and went to the park. I helped Dad in the garden.

But some things were different.

We didn't watch fireworks with Uncle Joe on the Fourth of July. We didn't go to the state fair with him or roast marshmallows in his backyard.

Sometimes I pretended Uncle Joe was just on a trip. I wrote letters and drew pictures for him. I kept everything in a special folder.

Dear Uncle Joe,
Today was a
hard day. I
thought about
you a lot.

Dear Uncle Joe,

There are a lot of ways to express your feelings about a loved one. You could make art projects or write letters or poems. You could sing the person's favorite songs or go to a place that holds good memories.

19

One Sunday night, just before school started again, the doorbell rang. There was Aunt Kay. Our Sunday sundaes were on again!

Life changes when a loved one dies. But moving on doesn't mean forgetting. Your loved one will always be a part of you.

We all miss Uncle Joe. We miss his loud laugh and his piggyback rides. But we still have fun.

I think I'd rather miss Uncle Joe than forget about him—even if it hurts sometimes.

Today *is* Uncle Joe's birthday.

It's been almost a year since he died. Aunt Kay is throwing a party to celebrate his life. We're going to light candles and tell stories and dance to his favorite music. There will be cake and balloons too.

I can't wait!

Glossary

afterlife—the idea that people live on in some way after their bodies die

casket—a wooden or metal box that holds a dead body and is buried in the ground; a coffin

cemetery—a place where people or animals are buried; a graveyard

cremation—the process of exposing a body to high heat so that it turns into ashes

funeral—a ceremony for someone who has died; a funeral usually takes place a short time after the death, and the body is present (*see* memorial service)

grief—the process we go through when we experience death or another kind of loss; when we grieve, we might feel sadness, anger, loneliness, and other emotions

memorial service—a ceremony for someone who has died; the service might take place many days or weeks after the death, and the body is not present (*see* funeral)

stroke—the sudden breaking of a blood vessel in the brain; strokes don't always lead to death

visitation—the time before a funeral during which people can offer comfort to the dead person's family and view the body; also called a wake

Read More

Brown, Laurie Krasny, and Marc Brown. *When Dinosaurs Die: A Guide to Understanding Death.* Boston: Little, Brown: 1996.

Buscaglia, Leo. *The Fall of Freddie the Leaf: A Story of Life for All Ages.* Thorofare, N.J.: C.B. Slack, 1982.

Crowe, Carole. *Turtle Girl.* Honesdale, Penn.: Boyds Mills Press, 2008.

Internet Sites

FactHound offers a safe, fun way to find Internet sites related to this book. All of the sites on FactHound have been researched by our staff.

Here's all you do:

Visit *www.facthound.com*

Type in this code: 9781404866775

 Check out projects, games and lots more at www.capstonekids.com

Index

after death, 13

crying, 5, 7, 13, 15

expressing feelings, 14, 19

fears, 10–11, 14, 16–17

funerals

   going to, 12–13

   planning, 9

hearing the news, 4–5, 6–7

memorial services, 9

remembering the loved one, 19, 20, 21, 22

seeing the loved one's body, 10–11

visitations, 10–11

visitors, 8–9

Look for all the books in the Life's Challenges series:

Good-bye, Jeepers

The Night Dad Went to Jail

Saying Good-bye to Uncle Joe

Weekends with Dad

Thanks to our advisers for their expertise, research, and advice:

Michele Goyette-Ewing, PhD
Director of Psychology Training
Yale Child Study Center

Terry Flaherty, PhD
Professor of English
Minnesota State University, Mankato

Editor: Jill Kalz
Designer: Alison Thiele
Art Director: Nathan Gassman
Production Specialist: Sarah Bennett
The illustrations in this book were created with collage and enhanced digitally.

Picture Window Books
1710 Roe Crest Drive
North Mankato, MN 56003
www.capstonepub.com

Library of Congress Cataloging-in-Publication Data
Loewen, Nancy, 1964–
  Saying good-bye to Uncle Joe : what to expect when someone you love
dies / by Nancy Loewen ; illustrated by Christopher Lyles.
    p. cm. — (Life's challenges)
  ISBN 978-1-4048-6677-5 (library binding)
  1. Children and death—Juvenile literature. 2. Bereavement in
children—Juvenile literature. 3. Grief in children—Juvenile
literature. I. Lyles, Christopher, 1977– II. Title. III. Series.

  BF723.D3L64 2012
  155.9'37—dc22   2011007457

Printed in the United States of America in North Mankato, Minnesota.
042013   007266R